ideals

CHRISTMAS

Vol. 48, No. 8

Publisher, Patricia A. Pingry
Editor, Nancy J. Skarmeas
Associate Editor, D. Fran Morley
Art Director, Patrick McRae
Contributing Editors, Marty Sowder Brooks, Lansing Christman, Deana Deck, Russ Flint, Pamela Kennedy
Editorial Assistant, LaNita Kirby

ISBN 0-8249-1095-8

IDEALS—Vol. 48, No. 8 December MCMXCI IDEALS (ISSN 0019-137X) is published eight times a year: February, March, May, June, August, September, November, December by IDEALS PUBLISHING CORPO-RATION, P.O. Box 148000, Nashville, Tenn. 37214. Second-class postage paid at Nashville, Tennessee, and additional mailing offices. Copyright © MCMXCI by IDE-ALS PUBLISHING CORPORATION. POSTMASTER: Send address changes to Ideals, Post Office Box 148000, Nashville, Tenn. 37214-8000. All rights reserved. Title IDEALS registered U.S. Patent Office.

SINGLE ISSUE—$4.95
ONE-YEAR SUBSCRIPTION—eight consecutive issues as published—$19.95
TWO-YEAR SUBSCRIPTION—sixteen consecutive issues as published—$35.95
Outside U.S.A., add $6.00 per subscription year for postage and handling.

The cover and entire contents of IDEALS are fully protect-ed by copyright and must not be reproduced in any man-ner whatsoever. Printed and bound in U.S.A.

THE CHRISTMAS GIFT FOR MOTHER from *WHEN DAY IS DONE* by Edgar A. Guest, copyright 1921 by The Reilly and Lee Company: Used by permission of the author's estate. DECEMBER by Edna Jaques: Used by permission of the author's estate. CANDLELIT HEART from *ROADS WIDE WITH WONDER* by Mary E. Linton: Used by permission of the author. FOR CHRISTMAS YEAR ROUND from *THE PRAYERS OF PETER MARSHALL*, compiled and edited by Catherine Marshall, copyright © 1949, 1950, 1951, 1954 by Catherine Marshall. Renewed 1982 by Catherine Marshall. Published by Chosen Books, Fleming H. Revell Company. Used by permission. Our special thanks to the following whose addresses we were unable to locate: Mary Hemeon Adkins for WHAT IS CHRISTMAS? Virginia Covey Boswell for THE LIGHTS OF HOME; Joy Belle Burgess for GOING HOME; Jo Geis for CHRISTMAS LONG AGO; Pauline Havard for CHRISTMAS; Earl A. Morris for CHRISTMASTIME AT OUR HOUSE; Faye Phillips Niles for WINTER WOODS SONG and Anton J. Stoffle for A CHRISTMAS OF LONG AGO.

Four-color separations by Rayson Films, Inc., Waukesha, Wisconsin

Printing by The Banta Company, Menasha, Wisconsin

The paper used in this publication meets the minimum requirements of American National Standard for Infor-mation Sciences—Permanence of Paper for Printed Library Materials, ANSI Z39.48-1984.

Inside covers
John Walters

Cover Photo
Bruno Pellegrini
International Stock Photo

Christmas

Pauline Havard

Christmas!
The scent of evergreens;
The tall Fir-tree, bright with tinsel,
  balls, and star;
The opening of the gifts, I see it all—
For memory holds my childhood's door ajar!

And so, though Time has made a gulf between
Each old, enchanted Christmas of the past
I smell the loved scent of the evergreen
And know the memory will always last—

A healing fragrance in the lonely night;
A glowing flame that keeps the heart alight.

Photo Opposite
COLORADO BLUE SPRUCE FARM
New Ringgold, Pennsylvania
Larry Lefever/Grant Heilman Photography

ICE-COVERED BERRIES
Libba Gillum, Photographer

Down an
Old Pathway

Lucille Crumley

I found some lovely things today
As I walked down an old pathway.
It was winter and the snow
Had fashioned the trees an ermine throw;

POINSETTIA
Bob Firth/Firth Photobank

Had carpeted the earth with white
And glittered it with diamonds bright;
Had frosted every shrub and weed
And blanketed each sleeping seed.
I saw the flash of feathered wings,
The blue of a Jay, a Cardinal that sings.
I saw child footprints in the snow,
It made me dream of long ago.
I found a lovely thing today.
I found peace down an old pathway.

5

Winter Woods Song

Faye Phillips Niles

The wind blows loud tonight and bitter cold;
The trees are bending, sighing like the seas,
Their leaves are fallen now in mounds of gold,
And all the woods are waiting for the freeze.

Safe under ice, bullfrogs will cease to croak,
And slumber on their muddy beds till spring;
Bare poplars soon will wear an ermine cloak:
White winter will bedight each living thing!

The pond will don a cap against the wind's blow;
Black bass inhabit frozen paradise;
The woods will be a fairyland of snow
When echoes wrap the silver hills of ice.

In company with wind and snow I'll walk,
My heart will sing with swaying stem and stalk.

Old Home Christmas

Christmas morning, complete with cookies;
Dad's coffee on the table;
Little children anxiously waiting for presents;
The Christ Child asleep in the stable.
Filling our hearts with excitement
    and great expectation;
Not knowing the sacrifice made,
Not realizing that the true gift of Christmas
Was in the manger where the Christ Child lay.

Warm Christmas memories fill our
    hearts as we grow
In our home rich with guidance and love;
Each of us learning the value of faith
In our blessed Savior, who's risen above.

Now each Christmas, our most precious gift
Is not what someone buys,
But seeing the beauty of our Savior's birth
From within our children's eyes.

Deborah Nudd Hines
Penn Yan, New York

Warm Christmas Memories

The snow is falling, white and cold
We sing of love and gifts of old.
It's Christmastime in our home town;
Not one tear or wayward frown
Is found here on Christmas eve.

The gifts are shaken in anticipation,
Awaited by wondering imaginations;
Carols are sung by strolling choirs
As bells are rung from steeple spires;
True love abounds for all to feel.

Apples, plums, pears, and cherries,
Chocolate cakes and warm blueberries,
Snow-cream made in fireplace light
To innocent eyes a great delight;
Sad, Christmas comes but once a year.

But when the Yule log is burning bright
On Christmas morning before first light,
Tiny feet scamper across the floor
Looking for traces of Santa's lore;
Awakening parents with squeals of joy.

Jim McConnell
Hendersonville, Tennessee

Reflections

The Miracle

Asleep in the stable lie the small lambs,
Nestled warm in the straw
  with the ewes and rams;
The ox dozes over his manger of hay,
And the sleeping calf dreams
  of meadows far away.

But here comes their master!
  The animals awake
And shake sleep from their eyes,
  this sight to partake;
For in walks a Woman, heavy with child,
Weary from wandering,
  yet at them she smiles.

The innkeeper leaves his lantern and goes
And one by one, shyly, each lamb arose
To watch, to see a Miracle start;
Something warm grows
  in each animal's heart.

A child is born! The ox leaves his manger
To give room for the Babe;
  He sleeps safe from danger;
Guarded by horns, now gentle, in the dim
Of the stable, in the barn of the inn.

The smallest of the lambs, so tiny and meek
Raises his head—is it to speak?
The ox feels it too, even the mice stir,
Doves rustle on the rafters with a soft whir.

Each gentle beast there feels that Divine Love,
From the tiny crouched mouse
  to the high perched dove,
And of one accord they begin to sing
In cherubic voices—such a wondrous thing!

"Glory to God in the Highest!" they say
"All praise be to Him
  who was born on this day.
Bless that King who was so humble
  He was able
To be born among animals
  in a Bethlehem stable.

Annie Glancy Chase
Milwaukee, Wisconsin

December

Edna Jaques

December takes on festive airs,
Angels walking unawares,
In and out our common doors,
Christmas carols in the store.
Bright-eyed children gaily clad,
Being, oh, so nice to dad.

Christmas concerts in the church,
Glowing logs of oak and birch
Burning in the polished grate;
Shiny apples on a plate,
Popcorn balls and taffy squares,
Loops of tinsel on the stairs.

Mother busy all day long,
On her lips a happy song
As she beats and stirs and bakes
Fat old-fashioned Christmas cakes,
Raisin cookies, doughnuts, ham,
Golden tarts with berry jam.

December is a joyful time,
Christmas bells that gaily chime,
Rosy cheeks and eyes aglow,
Starry skies and fields of snow—
'Tis no wonder that she wears,
Happy looks and festive airs.

Country Christmas

Elisabeth Weaver Winstead

Christmastime in the country,
What magic it is to be
Hanging wreaths of fragrant holly,
Bringing home the Christmas tree.

Handmade gifts with homespun flair,
Country dolls with braided hair,
Yarn stockings by the chimney hung,
On the doorstep, soft carols sung.

Sleigh bells jingling in the night,
Snowflakes falling, sparkling bright,
Mistletoe sprigs on mantel and door,
Peeking at presents, one moment more.

Fruitcakes baking and holiday pie,
Popcorn and eggnog for friends dropping by,
Plum pudding steaming in the pan,
Sweet, spicy smell of a gingerbread man.

Snuggled warmly in quilt-covered beds,
Wondrous dreams fill children's heads,
The countryside echoes a message of cheer:
Christmas peace and love in a joyous year.

ICE-COVERED ROAD
Near Grafton, Vermont
D'Arazien/Superstock

THE ROAD TO CHRISTMAS

Hilda Butler Farr

The road that leads to Christmas
Is lined with memory
Of holly wreaths and candles
And days that used to be.

The blessed joys of carols
That ring across the night,
The Baby in the manger,
A star our guiding light.

Beloved friends we treasure
Around a twinkling tree,
The road that leads to Christmas
Is lined with memory.

The Language of Snow

Emily Romano

On Christmas Eve the snowflakes fall
And swaddle all our world with white;
Even the wreath upon the door
Wears snowflakes for our soul's delight.

Each flake of snow has meaning now,
Each has a message to impart—
Upon this night of nights we see
Not with the eye, but with the heart.

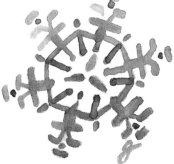

Country CHRONICLE
Lansing Christman

In a December of long ago, the snows were deep, the evergreens graced in pristine white, the boughs of oaks and maples gowned in snow. It covered fences and hedges and rooftops.

Diane, an eight-year-old country girl loved wintertime and snow, and the Christmas season. She wanted to share her joy, not only with family and friends, but with the birds who brightened the gray winter skies.

Diane took five large pine cones and spread soft peanut butter between the scales of each one. She rolled the cones in a mixture of sunflower and bird seeds. Finally, using a piece of string, and with her father's help, she hung the cones in trees outside her window.

Several mornings later she discovered one of her cones missing. Then another, and another, until all had gone, but not before she had learned the secret of their disappearance.

18

She saw a gray squirrel perch on a bough above the cone and then pull up the string, inch by inch, until it held the cone, peanut butter, seeds and all, in its front paws. While Diane watched from her window, the squirrel bit the string and released its holiday treat.

Diane could have been disappointed that the feast she had prepared for the chickadees, tufted titmice, nuthatches, and cardinals, had fallen into the paws of a squirrel. But when she saw the squirrel come down the tree, and scamper through the deep snow holding the cone straight out in its mouth like a man with a fat cigar, she smiled a Christmas smile. She realized that the squirrels, like the birds, were part of God's cre-

ation, and that they too should have a festive holiday.

I don't know if Diane continued preparing her holiday treats for the birds and squirrels in the years that followed that Christmas, but I imagine she did. I hope that today, she still sends greetings for a Merry Christmas to all of God's creatures.

The author of two published books, Lansing Christman has been contributing to Ideals *for almost twenty years. Mr. Christman has also been published in several American, foreign, and braille anthologies. He lives in rural South Carolina.*

19

TRIMMING THE TREE
Beerman/Superstock

Christmas at Our House

A. Earl Morris

It's Christmastime at our house,
A time of joy and cheer,
A time for which we watch and wait
The high point of the year.
The greeting cards the postman brings
Pile higher every day,
With love expressed in loveliness,
A truly thoughtful way.

CHRISTMAS COOKIES
W. Rousseau/Superstock

For weeks, it seems, there's been an air
Of glad and sweet suspense,
Of rustlings here and whispers there,
Expectancy intense.
Doors festooned with tinsel bright,
Arranged by loving hand,
For Christmastime has come again
To this, our happy band.

Each has a place, each has a part
On this the Day of Days.
No wonder we, with hearts sincere,
Sing songs of joy and praise!

21

TRAVELER'S Diary

Nancy J. Skarmeas

Photos courtesy, Old Salem Restoration,
Winston-Salem, North Carolina

Christmas in Old Salem

One Saturday each December, the crisp, cold early winter air of Old Salem, North Carolina, fills with the spicy aroma of Moravian molasses cookies baking in Winkler Bakery and the sounds of the Salem Brass Band playing eighteenth-century hymns. It's Christmas in Old Salem, a wonderful festival of tribute to the most joyous of Christian holidays and to a group of early Americans who devoted their lives to spreading the Christian message.

Christmas is celebrated on a single day in December, but the restored city of Old Salem pays tribute to its Moravian founders year round with tours of the city's buildings and demonstrations of the Moravian way of life. Salem, from the Hebrew for "peace," was founded in 1766.

The twelve men who settled Salem came from Bethlehem, Pennsylvania; but the roots of their church and their people go back to a fifteenth-century Bohemian named John Hus.

Hus was a teacher at the University of Prague and a preacher at one of that city's largest churches. Bohemia, which along with its neighboring provinces Moravia and Slavakia would later become Czechoslovakia, was loyal to the Roman Catholic church; John Hus, however, was a reformer.

In 1457, Hus and a group of his followers founded the *Unitas Fratrum*—the Union of Brethren—and devoted themselves to implementing his reforms. Soon, however, Hus and his followers gave up hope of overall church reform and sought their own peace away from Roman authority.

The Moravians sailed to America with three clear purposes. First, they were devoted to mission work among the Indians. Second, they sought to spread their faith to the other white settlers in the colony. Their third purpose was a practical one; the Moravians were devoted to a system of common work for the common goal of supporting their missionary work.

The first Moravian settlement in Georgia was short-lived. They then traveled to Pennsylvania, where they founded the city of Bethlehem. The Pennsylvania settlements were a great success, so much so that they caught the attention of Earl Granville, owner of a vast tract of Carolina land who was looking for reliable settlers. At Granville's invitation, the Moravians founded a small colony in the Carolina wilderness and called it Salem, dedicated to "God and the service of our fellow man."

The Moravian way of life in Salem was structured and disciplined, but also peaceful and content. While some settlers were farmers, Salem was from the beginning a center for crafts and trades. Life in the settlement was not strictly communal—residents owned their own shops and made their own profits—but all social and professional life was regulated by the church, and the focus was, from the beginning, not on individual financial gain but on supporting the community's mission work.

This focus on community provided Salem's craftspeople with a constant and positive shared motivation. They flourished, transforming their simple missionary settlement into a center for crafts, from woodworking to carriage-making to bookbinding. Salem also produced America's first symphony orchestras and her first composers. The same motive drove the musicians as did the craftspeople. Music was a vital part of Moravian religious and social life; musicians and composers developed in service of community values.

Salem's original settlers established a pattern of work for the common good that has bridged the generations.

Today, although Old Salem is an historical restoration, the heritage of the Moravians remains the guiding principle of the staff. Crafts of the eighteenth and nineteenth centuries are still carried out here—blacksmithing, weaving, dyeing and more, all practiced as they were in Salem's early days. Winkler Bakery's cookies and breads are still baked in the old brick beehive ovens, and hymns are played on the same brass instruments that inspired Salem's first composers. The difference is that today volunteers from the community demonstrate the crafts, play the music, and lead the tours that teach travelers the history and message of the Moravians.

At Christmas, Old Salem is in its finest form, decorated and polished for the most wonderful celebration of the year. The city is beautiful in all seasons and attracts travelers throughout the year, but there can be no better time to celebrate Old Salem's heritage than at Christmastime, when we all try to recreate the spirit of a generous and faithful Christian community that Old Salem, North Carolina, has never lost.

Moravian Molasses Cookies

The Winkler Bakery is one of the most popular stops for tourists in the restored village of Old Salem in Winston-Salem, North Carolina, and these thin, crispy cookies are one of the reasons! Built in 1800, the bakery is still producing breads, cakes, and cookies daily in its wood-fired oven, identical to the one used more than 100 years ago. This recipe, straight from the bakery, makes seven or eight *pounds* of cookies! If you prefer, you can cut the recipe in half and still have plenty of these spicy, delicious cookies for your Christmas gift-giving.

1	pound light brown sugar
6	ounces margarine
6	ounces shortening
1	quart molasses (Puerto Rican, which is very dark)
2	rounded tablespoons soda
½	cup boiling water
4	pounds flour (approx.)
2	tablespoons cloves
2	tablespoons ginger
2	tablespoons cinnamon

Melt shortening and margarine until it bubbles and add to sugar. Stir in the molasses. Dissolve soda in boiling water and add to mixture. Sift in approximately 4 pounds flour. Add spices along with the flour.

The dough should be almost stiff enough to roll. Cover and let set overnight. Do not refrigerate. On a floured, cloth-covered board, roll dough as thin as possible. Cut with cookie cutters and place on a greased pan. Bake in a 275° oven for exactly 10 minutes. Let cookies cool before removing from pans.

MORAVIAN MOLASSES COOKIES
Courtesy Winkler Bakery
Old Salem, Winston-Salem, North Carolina
Photo by Gerald Koser

GOING HOME

Joy Belle Burgess

Just down another little road,
    and over another hill,
Just through a little quiet town
    and then our hearts will thrill—
        At being home!

It's just a few more minutes now
    no more we'll be away,
We'll look upon the old home place
    and this will be the day—
        That we'll be home!

At last we see the snowbound fields,
    the old familiar barn,

And there I see the lighted window
glowing with its charm
Guiding us home!

And there at the open door we see
the dearest folks on earth,
We'll smile and cry with happiness,
aglow like the fire's hearth.
At last we're home!

Let the church bells in the valley ring
for all on Christmas Day,
Pealing forth with joy for all.
We'll bow our heads to pray.
With thanks, we're home!

We'll have a sumptuous dinner here,
with friends to say "Hello!"
And love will fill each joyous hour
so deep within we'll know
We're home!

Do You Remember?

Phyllis C. Michael

Do you remember, oh, do you remember
A long ago Christmas night,
When you were just a tiny child
Standing in the candlelight?

Standing with eyes that sparkled and glowed
As you gazed at the Christmas tree?
Do you remember, oh, do you remember
How grand this used to be?

The silver balls and the blue ones, dotting
The huge pine branches of green?
The strings of snow-white popcorn
Made lacy ruffles between?

The cranberry ropes of red near the bottom?
Your hands had draped them there.
Do you remember, oh, do you remember
Ever a scene more fair?

The smell of Christmas was in the parlor,
The sleighbells jingled outside;
Was there ever a moment
  so filled with rapture
Around the world so wide?

HAND-MADE ORNAMENTS
Gene Ahrens, Photographer

BITS & PIECES

'Twas the night before Christmas,
  when all through the house
Not a creature was stirring,
  not even a mouse;
The stockings were hung
  by the chimney with care,
In hopes that St. Nicholas
  soon would be there.

A Visit from St. Nicholas
Clement C. Moore

The Christ-child lay on Mary's lap,
His hair was like a light.
(O weary, weary were the world,
But here is all aright.)

The Christ-child stood at Mary's knee,
His hair was like a crown,
And all the flowers looked up at Him
And all the stars looked down.

Gilbert K. Chesterton

Somehow, not only for Christmas
  But all the long year through,
The joy that you give to others
  Is the joy that comes back to you;
And the more you spend in blessing
  The poor and lonely and sad,
The more of your heart's possessing
  Returns to make you glad.

John Greenleaf Whittier

30

O Come, all ye faithful,
Joyful and triumphant,
O come ye, O come ye
 to Bethlehem.
Come and behold Him,
Born, the King of Angels.

O come, let us adore Him.
O come, let us adore Him.
O come, let us adore Him,
Christ, the Lord.

John Francis Wade

Heap on more wood!—the wind is chill;
But let it whistle as it will,
We'll keep our Christmas merry still.

Sir Walter Scott

. . . it was always said of him,
that he knew how to keep Christmas well,
if any man alive possessed the knowledge.
May that be truly said of us, and all of us!
And so, as Tiny Tim observed,
"God Bless Us, Every One!"

A Christmas Carol
Charles Dickens

It came upon a midnight clear,
That glorious song of old,
From angels bending near the earth,
To touch their harps of gold;

Peace on the earth, good will to men,
From heaven's all gracious King;
The world in solemn stillness lay
To hear the angels sing.

Edmund H. Sears

I heard the bells on Christmas Day
Their old familiar carols play,
And wild and sweet the words repeat
Of peace on earth, good will to men!

Henry Wadsworth Longfellow

31

CRAFTWORKS

Handkerchief Angel

Marty Sowder Brooks

Here is a delightful, simple, and versatile little angel for your holiday decorating. She can be a centerpiece, as shown here, top a Christmas tree, or grace a wreath.

Materials Needed:
1 man's white handkerchief (16 inches square)
$1\frac{1}{2}$-inch round styrofoam ball
Florist wire
Black, fine point permanent marker
Hot glue gun or thick craft glue
Spanish moss
4-inch piece of lace or eyelet trim
$\frac{1}{2}$-yard gold paper ribbon
1 gold metallic pipe cleaner
8-inch styrofoam cone
Silk Christmas greenery

Directions:
1. Iron handkerchief to remove all crease lines.

2. Place the styrofoam ball in the center of the handkerchief and gather the fabric around the ball snugly. Secure it with a 6-inch piece of florist wire, wrapping so that the ends are at the back of the head. Do not clip the ends off.

3. With the permanent marker, draw the angel's closed eyes and smile.

4. Cover the scalp and hairline areas with glue and press on small, smooth clumps of Spanish moss to form the angel's hair. Check for bald spots and clip off any "wild hairs." Wrap the piece of lace trim around the angel's neck and secure the ends with glue.

5. Fold the gold paper ribbon to find the mid-point and overlap the ends at that point. Crimp the ribbon into a bow-tie shape to make the angel's wings and secure with the florist wire ends.

6. Make a halo by twisting the pipe cleaner into a small circle, leaving a short stem. Glue the stem to the back of the head.

7. To form the angel's hands, take one front corner of the handkerchief and tie a small, tight knot, leaving about $\frac{1}{2}$ inch of fabric. Tie a similar knot at the opposite corner of the handkerchief.

8. Bring the handkerchief knots together and glue together to resemble praying hands; let dry. Snip off the tail ends of the knots; glue the hands into position about 1 inch below the angel's chin.

9. To make the centerpiece as shown, slip the finished angel over the styrofoam cone and secure with a straight pin. Fasten the silk greenery to the base of the cone.

Photo by Gerald Koser

FROM MY
G·A·R·D·E·N
JOURNAL

Deana Deck

Christmas Amaryllis

The amaryllis, unquestionably beautiful in bloom, is not only a popular holiday gift plant but one that's full of surprises. Usually when purchased or received as a gift, the amaryllis is already in full bud, if not in actual bloom. It's not until after the bloom has died back, leaving what appears to be a very dead bulb, that the amaryllis pulls off its first surprise.

Suddenly long, straplike leaves shoot up, very quickly becoming a quite attractive foliage plant. A few short months later, with no warning at all, the foliage dies back and once again it would appear that the time has come to chuck the barren pot into the shed to be recycled.

Not so; this jokester of a bulb has yet another trick up its sleeve. As if by magic, a stalk makes a sudden appearance. It grows so quickly, it seems to happen before your eyes; and when it has reached its full, regal height of two to three feet, it produces not just one bloom but, in most cases, four or more.

This is an amazing plant, and one of the most amazing things about it is that it requires so little assistance to get through its complicated life cycle year in and year out. Keep it watered and reasonably well-nourished; keep it in a well-lit spot and it will just come and go indefinitely.

In just about all parts of the country the amaryllis is a houseplant. Only in southern Florida and other tropical areas can it be grown outdoors, although it does have a few cousins that duplicate its growth habits and are fun to have in the garden. None of them are named amaryllis, however; and as a matter of fact, neither is the amaryllis! The plant we call by that name is actually the *Hippeastrum* and is also known as the Barbados lily (that should give you an indication of its tropical origins).

Among its hardier cousins is a summer-blooming lily that produces shell-pink flowers that linger up to two weeks. This plant, known as the Resurrection lily, Surprise lily, Naked Lady or August lily, belongs to the Lycoris family and is known to botanists as *Lycoris squamigera*.

There is yet another cousin, *Lycoris radiata*, (also sometimes listed as *Amaryllis radiata*), that has the same growth habit but blooms in colors ranging from pink to red. All share a common growth habit: a bulb produces foliage which eventually dies back, to be replaced several weeks later by a single, tall, strong stalk which soon produces three or four huge, perfectly formed lily-shaped blooms.

The fact that these plants all share similar characteristics with the *Hippeastrum* we know as "amaryllis" has led to the habit of commonly referring to them all as amaryllis. In reality, the only true amaryllis in the garden is the fragrant Belladonna lily (*A. belladona*). Like its *lycoris* cousin, it has also been nicknamed the Naked Lady. It is hardy to Zone 5 (-10 to -20°) so can be grown outdoors in many parts of the country if placed in a warm sunny spot and mulched heavily in winter. The plant produces clusters of six to twelve blooms atop its stalk.

All amaryllis cousins can be container grown and do best in a mixture of one part potting soil to one part peat moss and one part perlite or sharp sand. In each case the bulb should be planted so that its upper tip is above the soil line. Water the plant well when potting it and then withhold water until foliage begins to appear. After the foliage dies back, reduce watering until the bloom stalk begins growing, then keep the plant moist until a month after the blossoms fade. Again, let the plant dry out between waterings until the foliage reappears. Water regularly during these periods of active growth and blooming and feed with liquid fertilizer once a month and you will be rewarded with spectacular blooms for many years.

Don't be disappointed if your Christmas amaryllis sets up a cycle of bloom that doesn't coincide with the holidays. Holiday plants, forced into early bloom by commercial growers, will revert back to their natural rhythm in time, surprising you with blooms in late winter or early spring. It's worth the wait!

Deana Deck lives in Nashville, Tennessee, where her garden column is a regular feature in the Tennessean.

35

Christmas Long Ago

Jo Geis

Frosty days and ice-still nights,
Fir trees trimmed with tiny lights,
Sound of sleigh bells in the snow,
That was Christmas long ago.

Tykes on sleds and shouts of glee,
Icy-window filigree,
Sugarplums and candle glow,
Part of Christmas long ago.

Footsteps stealthy on the stair,
Sweet-voiced carols in the air,
Stockings hanging in a row,
Tell of Christmas long ago.

Starry nights so still and blue,
Good friends calling out to you,
Life, so fast, will always slow . . .
For dreams of Christmas long ago.

Give Me an Old-Fashioned Christmas

Harriet Whipple

Give me an old-fashioned Christmas
With the ground all covered with snow;
When all those who roam, shall try to get home
No matter how far they must go.
Give me a bright cozy kitchen
With everyone busy and gay;
Where it smells so nice with foods that entice,
Each a favorite for Christmas day.
Give me the family all together,
Each one in their usual place,
Where the feasting is done
   with much cheer and fun
And a smile upon each face.

Give me a Christmas where folks drop in,
Where there're moments to reminisce;

Where there're children about
  to laugh and to shout
And plenty of holiday bliss.
Give me a tree from the forest
That is fresh and fragrant and green;
One trimmed with delight till it's
    festive and bright
And really quite splendid to see,
Where family tradition is followed
And loved as the holiday nears.
Every trinket and ball is cherished by all
And treasured throughout the years.

Give me a Christmas with gifts of love
Though they might be simple and small;
When folks really care and kind thoughts are there
I surely shall treasure them all.
Give me a Christmas where love abounds
And Christ is the honored guest,
Where the church bells ring and people all sing
And the day is specially blessed.
Give me a Christmas so pleasant
That it shall remain in my heart,
And in each future year when memories appear
It shall be a Christmas apart.

Christmas Past

Carice Williams

Each Christmas I remember
The ones of long ago;
I see our mantelpiece adorned
With stockings in a row.

Each Christmas finds me dreaming
Of days that used to be,
When we hid presents,
   here and there,
For all the family.

Each Christmas I remember
The fragrance in the air,
Of roasting turkey and mince pies
And cookies everywhere.

Each Christmas finds me longing
For Christmases now past,
And I am back in childhood
As long as memories last.

RUSTIC CHRISTMAS LIVING ROOM
Jessie Walker, Photographer

COLLECTOR'S CORNER

Karen S. Hodge

Madonna and Child Christmas Stamps

1981 Botticelli's *Madonna and Child*

The beginning of a rewarding and colorful collection is waiting for you each fall at your local post office. Since 1962, the U.S. Postal Service has been issuing stamps commemorating the Christmas season; and since 1970 they have issued at least two different designs each year. One design celebrates the secular and seasonal aspect of the holiday, but the other celebrates the religious theme of the season. Angels and the Nativity have been portrayed on Christmas stamps, but the most popular theme seems to be the Madonna and Child. In fact, every year since 1978 the Postal Service has issued a new Madonna and Child Christmas stamp.

The art for the Madonna and Child stamp is not a newly created work, but rather it is a reproduction from some of the most well-known of the world's masterpieces. For instance, the very first Madonna Christmas stamp, issued in 1966, featured Mary and the infant Jesus from a painting by Flemish Renaissance painter Hans Memling. The stamp did not reproduce the complete painting, but only the detail of Mother and Child. The following year, this same stamp was reissued in a slightly larger size to feature more of the painting.

The original Memling masterpiece hangs in the National Gallery of Art in Washington, D.C., as do most of the originals chosen for the Madonna Christmas stamps. The Art Institute of Chicago, however, provided two Madonna and Child masterpieces: in 1981 a painting by Botticelli and in 1984 one by Italian artist Fra Filippo Lippi.

With so many Madonna and Child paintings by great artists over the centuries, selecting just one each year must be difficult. The final choice, however, is made by the U.S. Postal Service Citizen's Advisory Board which is composed of postal employees, museum art experts (including an authority on art from the National Gallery), and other private citizens. The post office announces its final selection each year in September and the stamp itself goes on sale in October.

The Advisory Board has twice gone outside of the "usual" painted masterpieces: in 1980 and again in 1985. In the first instance, the board chose as the Christmas Madonna stamp, a small portion of the Epiphany window in the Bethlehem Chapel in the Washington National Cathedral. As this cathedral has become known as the "Nation's Church," a detail from this window gracing a postage stamp seems appropriate. The second instance of a nontraditional Madonna was the selection of the *Genoa*

42

Epiphany window, Bethlehem Chapel, Washington National Cathedral 1980

Serious stamp collectors recommend displaying the stamps in specially designed stamp albums or photo albums with soft, plastic pockets. If the stamp is attached to a very old envelope, or if the city of cancellation is important to the collector, both should be saved. If the envelope is new or of no sentimental value to the collector, carefully cut around the stamp and throw away the envelope. Another attractive way to show off the rich colors of the Madonna stamps is to frame several, grouping them by artist or by colors of the stamps. Either grouping makes a lovely collage which can be displayed all year round.

With the issue of new Christmas stamps every year, this collection is sure to grow; but don't expect to grow rich from this collection. Because of the popularity of the stamps and the large quantity produced by the post office, even the older Madonna Christmas stamps are rarely worth more than three or four times their face value. The intangible rewards of such a collection, however, are many; the meaning of the subject, the richness of the colors, and the history of the paintings all combine to make Christmas Madonna stamps unique and inspiring collectibles.

Photos courtesy The American Philatelic Society

Madonna. This Madonna, from the Detroit Institute of Arts, is a marble sculpture by the Italian sculptor Luca della Robbia. The pure white Madonna pictured against a dark blue background made a sharp contrast to the rich multitude of colors in the many painted masterpieces which have gone before and which have come after.

The vivid and varied color of the Madonna stamps is their main appeal to collectors of these beautiful stamps; and their display should be handled so as to enjoy their beauty to its utmost.

Luca della Robbia's *Genoa Madonna* 1985

Hans Memling's *Madonna and Child* 1966

43

A Christmas of Long Ago

Anton J. Stoffle

Oh, give me a Christmas of long ago,

With a heartfelt warmth and a candle's glow.

Bring back the scenes so gorgeous to see,

The family sitting around the tree.

Let me enjoy the carols and songs,

Going to church with the Christmas-eve crowds.

Treat me once more with those cookies and cakes,

Delicious dinners Aunt Nell used to make.

Just let me sit in the merry old sleigh,

Tug at the reins, and then, "Donner, away!"

Place me amidst all my jolly old friends,

Laughing, rejoicing till the season ends.

Blessings of peace and good will on earth,

Honoring thoughts of the dear Savior's birth.

Oh, give me the Christmas that used to be,

Like the one I see here in my memory.

COUNTRY CHRISTMAS BUFFET
Jessie Walker, Photographer

A SLICE OF LIFE

Edgar A. Guest

The Christmas Gift for Mother

In the Christmas times of the long ago,
There was one event we used to know
  That was better than any other;
It wasn't the toys that we hoped to get,
But the talks we had—and I hear them yet—
  Of the gifts we'd buy for Mother.

If ever love fashioned a Christmas gift,
Or saved its money and practiced thrift,
  'Twas done in those days, my brother—
Those golden times of Long Gone By,
Of our happiest years, when you and I
  Talked over the gift for Mother.

46

We hadn't gone forth on our different ways
Nor coined our lives into yesterdays
   In the fires that smelt and smother,
And we whispered and planned in our youthful glee
Of that marvelous "something" which was to be
   The gift of our hearts to Mother.

It had to be all that our purse could give,
Something she'd treasure while she could live,
   and better than any other.

We gave it the best of our love and thought,
And, Oh, the joy when at last we'd bought
   That marvelous gift for Mother!

Now I think as we go on our different ways,
Of the joy of those vanished yesterdays.
   How good it would be, my brother,
If this Christmas-time we could only know
That same sweet thrill of the Long Ago
   When we shared in the gift for Mother.

Edgar A. Guest began his illustrious career in 1895 at the age of fourteen when his work first appeared in the Detroit Free Press. *His column was syndicated in over 300 newspapers, and he became known as "The Poet of the People."*

47

Read to Me

Art by Russ Flint

Jesus, Our Brother

An old carol from France

Jesus our brother, kind and good,
Was humbly born in a stable rude;
The friendly beasts around Him stood,
Jesus our brother, kind and good.

"I," said the donkey, shaggy and brown,
"I carried His mother
   up hill and down;
I carried her safely to Bethlehem town,
I," said the donkey, shaggy and brown.

"I," said the cow, all white and red,
"I gave Him my manger for His bed;
I gave Him my hay to pillow His head.
I," said the cow, all white and red.

"I," said the sheep with the curly horn,
"I gave Him my wool for a blanket warm.
He wore my coat on Christmas morn.
I," said the sheep with the curly horn.

"I," said the dove from the rafters high,
"I cooed Him to sleep so He would not cry,
I cooed Him to sleep, my mate and I.
I," said the dove from the rafters high.

And every beast, by some good spell,
In the stable dark was glad to tell,
Of the gift he gave Immanuel,
The gift he gave Immanuel.

48

nd in the
sixth month the angel Gabriel was sent from God
unto a city of Galilee, named Nazareth,
To a virgin espoused to a man whose name was Joseph,
of the house of David; and the virgin's name was Mary.
And the angel came in unto her, and said,
Hail, thou that art highly favoured,
the Lord is with thee:
blessed art thou among women.

And the angel said unto her, Fear not, Mary:
for thou hast found favour with God.
And, behold, thou shalt conceive in thy womb,
and bring forth a son, and shalt call his name JESUS.
He shall be great, and shall be called
the Son of the Highest: and the Lord God
shall give unto him the throne of his father David:
And he shall reign over the house of Jacob for ever;
and of his kingdom there shall be no end.

Luke 1: 26-28, 30-33

nd Mary arose in
those days, and went into the hill country with haste,
into a city of Juda; And entered
into the house of Zacharias,
and saluted Elisabeth. And it came to pass,
that, when Elisabeth heard the salutation of Mary,
the babe leaped in her womb;
and Elisabeth was filled with the Holy Ghost:

And she spake out with a loud voice,
and said, Blessed art thou among women,
and blessed is the fruit of thy womb.
And blessed is she that believed:
for there shall be a performance of those things
which were told her from the Lord.
And Mary said, My soul doth magnify the Lord,
and my spirit hath rejoiced
in God my Saviour.

Luke 1: 39-42, 45-47

Photo Opposite
THE VISITATION
St. Andrews's Church: Tecumseh, Nebraska
The Crosiers/Gene Plaisted, OSC, Photographer

nd it came to pass
in those days, that there went out a decree
from Caesar Augustus,
that all the world should be taxed.
And all went to be taxed, every one into his own city.
And Joseph also went up from Galilee,
out of the city of Nazareth, into Judea,
unto the city of David,
which is called Bethlehem;
(because he was of the house and lineage of David:)
To be taxed with Mary his espoused wife,
being great with child.

And so it was, that, while they were there,
the days were accomplished
that she should be delivered.
And she brought forth her firstborn son,
and wrapped him in swaddling clothes,
and laid him in a manger;
because there was no room for them in the inn.

Luke 1, 3-7

nd there were
in the same country shepherds abiding in the field,
keeping watch over their flock by night.
And, lo, the angel of the Lord came upon them,
and the glory of the Lord shone round about them:
and they were sore afraid.
And the angel said unto them, Fear not:
for, behold, I bring you good tidings of great joy,
which shall be to all people.
For unto you is born this day
in the city of David
a Saviour, which is Christ the Lord.
And this shall be a sign unto you;
Ye shall find the babe wrapped in swaddling clothes,
lying in a manger.

And suddenly there was with the angel
a multitude of the heavenly host praising God,
and saying, Glory to God in the highest,
and on earth peace, good will toward men.

Luke 2: 8-14

*nd it came to
pass, as the angels were gone away from them
into heaven, the shepherds said one to another,
Let us now go even unto Bethlehem,
and see this thing which is come to pass,
which the Lord hath made known unto us.*

*And they came with haste, and found Mary,
and Joseph, and the babe
lying in a manger.
And when they had seen it,
they made known abroad the saying
which was told them concerning this child.
And all they that heard it
wondered at those things
which were told them by the shepherds.
And the shepherds returned,
glorifying and praising God
for all the things that they had heard and seen,
as it was told unto them.*

Luke 2: 15-18, 20

hen Herod,
when he had privily called the wise men . . .
sent them to Bethlehem, and said,
Go and search diligently for the young child;
and when ye have found him, bring me word again,
that I may come and worship him also.

When they had heard the king, they departed;
and, lo, the star, which they saw in the east,
went before them, till it came
and stood over where the young child was.
When they saw the star, they rejoiced
with exceeding great joy.
And when they were come into the house,
they saw the young child with Mary his mother,
and fell down, and worshipped him:
and when they had opened their treasures,
they presented unto him gifts;
gold, and frankincense, and myrrh.

Matthew 2: 7-11

nd when
eight days were accomplished
for the circumcising of the child,
his name was called JESUS,
which was so named of the angel
before he was conceived in the womb.

And when the days . . . were accomplished,
they brought him to Jerusalem,
to present him to the Lord;
And to offer a sacrifice according to that
which is said in the law of the Lord,
A pair of turtledoves, or two young pigeons.
And, behold, there was a man in Jerusalem,
whose name was Simeon. . . .
And he came by the Spirit into the temple:
and when the parents brought in the child Jesus . . .
then took he up in his arms, and blessed God,
and said, Lord, now lettest thou thy servant depart in peace
. . . For mine eyes have seen thy salvation,
Which thou hast prepared before the face of all people. . . .

Luke 2: 21-22, 24-31

62

ehold, the
angel of the Lord appeareth to Joseph
in a dream, saying, Arise,
and take the young child and his mother,
and flee into Egypt, and be thou there
until I bring thee word:
for Herod will seek the young child
to destroy him.

When he arose, he took the young child
and his mother by night, and departed into Egypt:
And was there until the death of Herod:
that it might be fulfilled
which was spoken of the Lord by the prophet,
saying, Out of Egypt have I called my son.

Matthew 2: 13-15

Photo Opposite
THE FLIGHT
Church of the Nativity: St. Paul, Minnesota
The Crosiers/Gene Plaisted, OSC, PHotographer

THROUGH MY WINDOW

Pamela Kennedy

A Magi's Quest

Kaspar was weary, dreadfully weary. The hot air trembled above the baking earth. The camels, like dusty vessels on a sandy sea, rocked back and forth monotonously. How long had he been traveling? It seemed ages ago he and his two companions had departed Persia upon this quest.

The steadfast rhythm of the camel carried Kaspar's thoughts back. As students of the stars and holy writings, Kaspar and his fellow Magi studied their ancient manuscripts and astrological charts for unusual signs and portents. One day they came upon an intriguing sentence written by the ancient prophet, Balaam: "There shall come a star out of Jacob and a scepter shall arise out of Israel." Excited by their discovery, Kaspar and his fellow Magi eagerly searched for further information.

It was Kaspar who stumbled upon the message in the ancient Hebrew writings of Daniel: "Know, therefore, and understand that from the going forth of the commandment to restore Jerusalem, unto the Anointed One, the Prince, the time shall be seven and threescore and two weeks." Their hearts pounding, the Magi computed the symbolic weeks of years and came to the conclusion that the promised king was to appear that very year!

Night after night, they scanned the evening sky for signs of a new phenomenon; a comet, perhaps, or a new star, until one still evening, shortly after sunset, they saw it! Gleaming with blue-white fire, rising above the horizon, a new, bright star quivered in the purple sky.

Without further discussion, the Magi prepared for a long journey, and headed off across the trackless lands to the west.

They passed through fertile valleys and over windswept mountains, in frigid cold and sweltering heat, but they never talked of turning back. The star, as steadfast as their wills, beckoned them on.

"Kaspar, look there!" Malchior's cry jarred Kaspar from his reflections and he followed his companion's outstretched arm. There before them lay the silver thread of the River Jordan, winding through a fertile valley green with cedars. They urged their lumbering mounts on, across the ford and on to the city of Jerusalem.

There they found lodging and requested an audience with King Herod, hoping to discover the whereabouts of the royal heir they sought.

After several days, the Magi received word to come to Herod's magnificent palace.

"My advisers tell me you have been inquiring after a certain baby, born to be the king of the Jews," Herod began.

"Yes, your majesty," Kaspar replied. "You see we have seen his star."

Herod raised a jeweled hand to silence Kaspar. "Yes, well, I have had my own scribes investigate such Scriptures and have learned this royal one you seek is to be born in Bethlehem—an insignificant town just to the south."

At the news, Kaspar caught his breath.

"You will go as my emissaries," Herod continued, "and when you find the child you will inform me that I, too, may go and worship him." A smile played across the royal lips and Kaspar thought of a desert cobra about to strike.

He dropped his eyes from Herod's and nodded slightly. "It is as your majesty says," he replied, and the monarch dismissed them with an imperious wave of the hand.

Excitedly the Magi set out for the city of David. The familiar star moved ahead of them again, beckoning them on through the darkness until it stopped above a small house in Bethlehem.

Kaspar knocked softly on the wooden door. Slowly, it opened and a man greeted Kaspar and his companions.

"Shalom," the stranger said.

"We have come from afar," Kaspar explained. "We have followed the star in search of the infant king foretold for centuries in the Ancient Writings."

The man at the door moved aside and motioned for the Magi to enter. Then he beckoned them toward a small room at the rear of the house.

The soft light of the single star streamed down upon a young woman holding a sleeping baby.

Kaspar and the others stood in awe, then one by one, they sank to their knees offering the priceless gifts they had carried all these months: gold, frankincense, myrrh. Once the gifts had seemed grand; now they paled before the mother and child. As they watched, the baby stirred, waved a tiny arm, yawned, then looked into Kaspar's eyes.

Wonder filled Kaspar's breast. An understanding beyond words flashed in his mind, and he fell on his face before the tiny child.

Later, he could not recall how long he lay there, prostrate, worshipping. When he stood to leave, however, he was aware of a change deep within his soul. Kaspar knew he had glimpsed the face of God and he would never be the same. Peace flooded his heart and a sense of urgency drove him to depart at once—not to return to Herod's court, but to carry the news home to Persia.

Kaspar could not wait to share the outcome of the Quest. Finally he had discovered Truth. It was the Truth of God's choosing, not man's. It was the Truth of the Divine becoming flesh in an eternal mystery of love.

Pamela Kennedy is a freelance writer of short stories, articles, essays, and children's books. Married to a naval officer and mother of three children, she has made her home on both U.S. coasts and in Hawaii and currently resides in Washington, D.C. She draws her material from her own experiences and memories, adding bits of imagination to create a story or mood.

CHRISTMAS WREATH
Lancaster, Pennsylvania
Larry Lefever/Grant Heilman Photography

The Lights of Home

Virginia Covey Boswell

When Christmas snows are falling soft
Upon December hills,

68

CHRISTMAS WREATH
G. Glod/Superstock

Although I've chosen roads to roam,
My heart retakes the path toward home.

When Christmas dawns upon the world
And logs have lit the hearth,
My heart remembers tender care
Because the lights of home were there.

69

LEGENDARY AMERICANS

Pearl Buck

Christmas was a truly magical time for young Pearl Buck. The daughter of American missionaries in China, Pearl left her native country at the age of three months and grew up much as a typical Chinese child. She spoke the Chinese language, followed Chinese custom and tradition, ate Chinese food, and attended school and played with Chinese friends.

Except at Christmastime. On December twenty-fifth, Pearl and her small family were Americans. They decorated a tree, exchanged gifts, feasted on turkey, and celebrated the birth of a tiny baby in a Bethlehem manger. Pearl's parents told stories of Christmas in their native Virginia and these wonderful, idealized memories became Pearl's vision of her native country.

Pearl's parents gave her a priceless gift with each of these childhood Christmases, for they instilled in her a love for the native country she had never seen. But they had given her an even greater gift at the age of three months, when they took her away from that country. Pearl Buck grew up without the normal experiences and advantages of American children of her day; but by birth a member of one culture, by experience a member of another, she was accepted with kindness and goodwill by both and, in turn, she accepted both equally and without prejudice.

Pearl Buck often said that she had always known she would be a writer and had simply waited until she had something to write about to begin. She found her subject in the gift given to her by her parents: Chinese culture. *The Good Earth*, her first novel, was a simple story of the common life of Chinese peasants.

Buck had her doubts about the novel from the start. She wondered whether Western audiences could identify with these characters so remote from themselves. Her doubts were unfounded. Americans read *The Good Earth*, and in the process learned about Chinese life, and learned that although the language, customs, and history were different, the people themselves were human and recognizable.

Pearl Buck's novels and stories brought the life and people of China to America and to the rest of the western world. She was awarded great praise and countless awards, including both the Pulitzer and Nobel prizes. But her love for the culture of her youth inspired her to give another gift, perhaps even greater for its profound and permanent impact on the lives of the receivers.

Throughout her life, Pearl Buck had a special place in her heart for children. She had one child of her own, and adopted five others. Knowing this, and also knowing her love for Asian culture, a friend of Buck's called her one Christmastime with a very special request. Could she find a home for a half-Chinese, half-American baby rejected by both sides of his family?

It was Christmas on Buck's Pennsylvania farm, a time she had made as special for her own children as her parents had done for her in China. She gathered her family around her and asked their advice on the plight of the unwanted baby. Their decision was unanimous. Not only must they find a home for that child, they must make a home for him—their home. Thus began Welcome House, Inc., Pearl Buck's agency devoted to the placement of abandoned, cross-cultural babies. Over the years, Buck found homes for countless of these children, homes where their dual heritage was cherished, nurtured, and respected. In so doing, Buck brought the Chinese and American people one step closer, showing the Asian people that their neighbors across the world could be generous and open-hearted, and through these special children, allowing Americans to demonstrate their capacity to love without regard to race and national heritage.

Pearl Buck once wrote that "the doors that Christmas opens never close." Her own life proves the truth of her belief, for her experience consisted of a series of open doors—opened not only by one single day of celebration each December, but by a Christmas spirit of peace and goodwill never confined to a particular time or place. The missionary commitment of her parents opened to her the door to China, and she in turn used her literary talents to open this door to each one of her readers. And with Welcome House, the threshold of this doorway was crossed, and children otherwise forgotten found love, comfort, and safety. For these children, for the families that adopted them, and for every person their lives ever touched, the doors opened by Pearl Buck's love and kindness never again were closed.

71

Candlelit Heart

Mary E. Linton

Somewhere across the winter world tonight
You will be hearing chimes that fill the air;
Christmas extends its all-enfolding light
Across the distance . . . something we can share.

You will be singing, just the same as I,
These old familiar songs we know so well,
And you will see these same stars in your sky
And wish upon that brightest one that fell.

I shall remember you and trim my tree,
One shining star upon the topmost bough;
I will hang wreaths of faith that all may see—
Tonight I glimpse beyond the here and now.

And all the time that we must be apart
I keep a candle in my heart.

Photo Opposite
COUNTRY CHRISTMAS TREE
Jessie Walker, Photographer

50 YEARS AGO

Listen, The Great Organ!

People all over the United States this coming winter are to hear recitals over a radio network of music from an organ that has been 21 years in building. This instrument, privately owned, was built by John Hays Hammond, Jr. in his house at Gloucester, Mass. Mr. Hammond's thought has been from the first that when the organ was completed some way would be found to "lend" it to people everywhere who love music. Obviously someone would have to be the medium between the instrument and the listening public. Otherwise grim circumstances turned a kind face; for among those who fled France early in the war was Josef Bonnet, member of the family which has, for generations, ground the lenses that supply the beacons from the major lighthouses of the world. Himself a brilliant musician, during the spring and summer M. Bonnet made an album of pipe organ recordings. Late in the autumn M. Bonnet is to begin a series of regular broadcasts from Gloucester.

. . . The Huge instrument speaks into a room which is only 100 feet long by 60 feet high. A room of that size, through relatively a large room, is hardly to be called large in relation to an organ of more than 100 stops, divided into five separate choirs, each under separate expression. The obvious pitfall is that the organ could easily

74

bulge the acoustical seams; and in the fact that in no great cathedral, traditionally regarded as acoustically all but perfect for its celebrated organ, has the production of tone been comparable, some experts believe, with the balance and fusion which, by his handling of complex elements, Mr. Hammond has been able to secure. When we heard the organ played, we listened for a "smudging" on the fringes of sound such as are to be heard in sound produced by pipe organs in edifices of stone. A sound may hollow out, or jiggle at the edges of the tone, or reverberate, and we accept this "fringing" as one of the natural hazards. But from the merest string-choir murmur to the full organ power of the Hammond instrument, not a waver, not the shimmer of the tiniest reverberation could we detect.

Mr. Hammond is quick to disclaim the credit for the whole production. "Some of the greatest builders of the present day have contributed their pipes to this instrument," he says.

When Mr. Hammond designed his house, he designed the Great Hall—which is perhaps two thirds of the total bulk of the house—to house the Great Organ he meant eventually to design and build. Since a large part of the instrument speaks directly through the walls and vaulting, there were large problems of the handling of bulk and form.

Mr. Hammond made use of Greek vases, as in ancient Greek theaters, to subdue reverberations of sound in the amphitheaters. He had first observed the working of this system at the little Greek theater in Syracuse in Southern Italy. He built into the walls of his Gothic Great Hall absorption chambers approximating the Grecian idea, which would limit undue reverberations, especially of the hazardous lower-pedal notes. The result has been a satisfactory room for purposes of phonograph recording, amplification of sound for casual listening purposes and, now, broadcasting of music with the Great Organ.

from *The Christian Science Monitor*
November 8, 1941

75

What Is Christmas?

Mary Hemeon Adkins

Christmas is the night of nights,
Let us stir afar.
Filled with wonder, filled with love,
Searching for the star.

Christmas is the day of days,
Let us all rejoice.
Filled with reverence, filled with praise,
Sing with blessed voice!

Christmas is the time of times,
Let us praise again.
God has sent the world His son,
Peace on Earth. Amen!

LINDEN HALL CHAPEL
Lititz, Pennsylvania
Larry Lefever/Grant Heilman Photography

For Christmas Year Round

from *The Prayers of Peter Marshall*

"Oh come to my heart, Lord Jesus;
There is room in my heart for Thee."

Lord Jesus, we thank Thee for the spirit shed abroad in human hearts on Christmas. Even as we invited Thee on Christmas to be born again in our heart, so wilt Thou now go with us throughout the days ahead, to be our Companion in all that we do. Wilt Thou help each one of us to keep Christmas alive in our hearts and in our homes, that it may continue to glow, to shed its warmth, to speak its message during all the bleak days of winter.

May we hold to that spirit, that we may be as gentle and as kindly today as we were on Christmas Eve, as generous tomorrow as we were on Christmas morning.

Then if—by Thy help—we should live through a whole week in that spirit, it may be we can go into another week, and thus be encouraged and gladdened by the discovery that Christmas can last the year round.

So give us joyful, cheerful hearts to the glory of Jesus Christ, our Lord. Amen.

Readers' Forum

I have a Christmas story I would like to share with you.

I have Christmas Ideals, *Vol. 20, No. 6, November, 1963. This issue has been on our coffee table with a candle and a Bible every year since.*

Our daughter came home a week before Christmas for a day. My 91 year old mother is ill and . . . I had not decorated as much as usual and did not put our cherished Ideals *on the table.*

My daughter noticed this but said nothing. Christmas morning . . . I found a 1990 Christmas issue of Ideals. *A note enclosed said, "Mother, it did not seem like Christmas with our* Ideals *not on the coffee table, is it lost? Here is a new one for you."*

Mrs. William T. Preston
Kenova, West Virginia

I have been fortunate to receive several issues, as gifts, of your beautiful inspiring magazine. I have enjoyed them so much.

The one for Mother's Day really touched me. "The Store Bought Dress." I remember once my mother wasn't well enough to make me a dress so asked a friend to take me down town to buy me one. My mother made very lovely dresses for me, but the joy of going to a store and being able to choose my dress was almost inconceivable. I was so happy. It cost $1.98. You know how long ago that was. I'm now 86!

Light, love and blessings to you and your work.

Rietta Close Scofield
Woodbury, Connecticut

My first privilege is to say "Maholo Nui Loa"—thank you very much for the quality, tone and substance of Ideals *(aptly named indeed). I had missed it for 7 years in Hawaii, had almost forgotten what I was missing!*

Just keep giving us the same!

Grace B. Dunford
Salt Lake City, Utah

Editor's Note: We're sorry you missed receiving *Ideals* during your stay in Hawaii. Just a reminder to all—if *Ideals* is not available in your local bookstore, it can be delivered right to your door by subscription!

A CHRISTMAS BARN IN NORTHERN OHIO
Photograph by subscriber Kenneth Indoe of Lodi, Ohio

ideals®
Celebrating Life's Most Treasured Moments